AIGA/SF
EPHEMERA PHILATELICA

a stamp address book

CHRONICLE BOOKS
SAN FRANCISCO

The American Institute of Graphic Arts, founded in 1914, is the oldest and largest organization committed to the promotion of excellence in graphic design.
http://www.aigasf.org

AIGA/SF thanks Bill Senkus, whose philatelic passion inspired this project.
http://alphabetilately.home.att.net

Designed by Alethea Morrison
Cover art designed by Ken Cook
Printed in Hong Kong
Typeset in Garamond

ISBN 0-8118-2743-7

10 9 8 7 6 5 4 3 2 1

Distributed in Canada by
Raincoast Books
9050 Shaughnessy Street
Vancouver, B.C. V6P 6E5

Chronicle Books LLC
85 Second Street
San Francisco, CA 94105
www.chroniclebooks.com

THE ALLURE OF POSTAGE STAMPS

and philately (the term for the collection and study of stamps); the enduring importance of mail service in the daily lives of people everywhere; and the creativity of graphic design are all celebrated by the images in this address book. They were produced by graphic designers in AIGA/SF, the San Francisco Chapter of the American Institute of Graphic Arts, America's largest professional graphic design organization. After an A-to-Z list of philatelic terms had been compiled by Bill Senkus, Sheryn Labate, and Alyson Kuhn, designers at twenty-six Bay Area studios translated them into finished designs. Together, they explore a marvelous range of visual possibilities.

Postal systems operated in ancient cultures, including Babylon, Persia, and Rome. Cyrus, ruler of Persia, stationed horsemen at posts or stations located one day's ride apart. Delivering messages from one station to the next was called "post riding." These Persian post riders made an indelible impression upon the fifth-century B.C. Greek historian Herodotus, who wrote, "And neither snow nor rain nor heat nor gloom of night stays these couriers from the swift completion of their appointed rounds."

Although postal systems have existed for thousands of years, postage stamps are a relatively recent development. In the 1830s, English postage was calculated by a complex system based on the distance and the number of pages in a letter. Reformer Rowland Hill proposed the "penny post," permitting people to mail a half-ounce letter anywhere in the kingdom for a single penny.

Hill's innovations also included the world's first adhesive postage stamps, issued in 1840. Sporting a profile of Queen Victoria printed in black ink with the words "Postage" and "One Penny," these first stamps were denounced by the press. Licking stamps was called a surefire method of spreading the plague and an insult to Her Majesty by "slobbering all over her head." But stamps prevailed over their critics and were soon issued by postal systems around the world.

In a tradition dating to ancient coins, early stamps symbolized autocratic authority through profile portraits of political leaders. These early generic images were joined by commemoratives honoring anniversaries of people or events, and topicals whose illustrations depict flora, fauna, or other attractive subjects. People were fascinated by miniature masterpieces of the engraver's art arriving in the right-hand corner of letters and saved these perforated and gummed receipts of prepaid postage. Collecting stamps developed into a popular pastime, and philately became known as "the hobby of kings."

A rich vocabulary has evolved around postage stamps; for example, the term cinderella is used for stamp-sized graphics that look like stamps but have no value as postage. This brings us to the graphic art presented here: imaginative cinderellas presenting an illustrated alphabet of philatelic terms. Words like bisect, overprint, and setenant are expressed with originality and graphic wit. These pages are graced with a fascinating diversity of approaches, offering a fitting tribute to the visual vitality of postage stamps.

PHILIP B. MEGGS
School of Arts Research Professor,
Virginia Commonwealth University

A

A

is for

ADVERTISING COVERS

The junk mail of a century ago. Businesses dressed up their envelopes—back as well as front—with elaborate, colorful images. These covers provide a glimpse of the culture, commerce, and design of their era. Modern collectors love them, and many are quite valuable.

NAME

address

e-mail

phone | *fax*

NAME

address

e-mail

phone | *fax*

NAME

address

e-mail

phone | *fax*

NAME

address

e-mail

phone *fax*

NAME

address

e-mail

phone *fax*

NAME

address

e-mail

phone *fax*

NAME

address

e-mail

phone *fax*

NAME

address

e-mail

phone *fax*

NAME

address

e-mail

phone *fax*

NAME

address

e-mail

phone *fax*

NAME

address

e-mail

phone *fax*

NAME

address

e-mail

phone *fax*

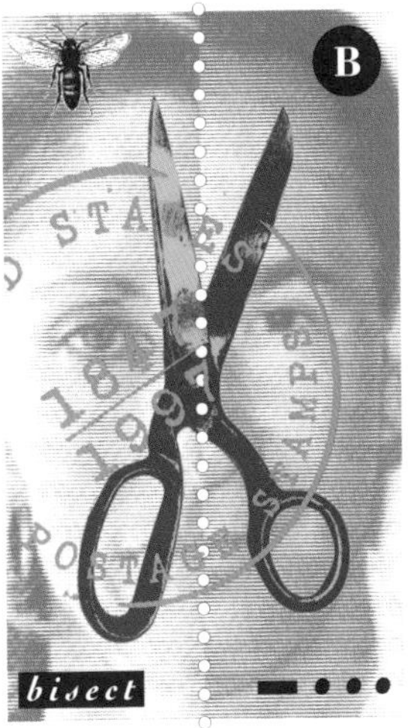
B
bisect

B

is for

BISECT

A postage stamp cut in half and used to pay half its face value. There are even trisects. This practice was tolerated until the 1870s, generally in times of shortage or other adversity. Do not try this today—it's illegal to cut, deface, or even overlap stamps on your mail.

Designed by Doug Akagi, Alison McKee, Joanna Wiraatmadja, Christopher Simmons, Jason Oshiro; Akagi Remington, San Francisco.

NAME

address

e-mail

phone | *fax*

NAME

address

e-mail

phone | *fax*

NAME

address

e-mail

phone | *fax*

NAME

address

e-mail

phone | *fax*

NAME

address

e-mail

phone | *fax*

NAME

address

e-mail

phone | *fax*

NAME

address

e-mail

phone *fax*

NAME

address

e-mail

phone *fax*

NAME

address

e-mail

phone *fax*

NAME

address

e-mail

phone | *fax*

NAME

address

e-mail

phone | *fax*

NAME

address

e-mail

phone | *fax*

Cheval
PARIS
Couture pour Hommes

C

is for

CINDERELLA STAMP

The stepchild of the postage stamp. Call it a poster stamp, a Christmas seal, or a label. It looks like a stamp, but it won't carry the mail. Many are more elaborately designed than the postage stamps they emulate, and all are avidly sought by collectors. Some fetch princely prices.

Designed by Martha Newton Furman Design & Illustration, San Ramon, CA.

NAME

address

e-mail

phone *fax*

NAME

address

e-mail

phone *fax*

NAME

address

e-mail

phone *fax*

NAME

address

e-mail

phone *fax*

NAME

address

e-mail

phone *fax*

NAME

address

e-mail

phone *fax*

NAME

address

e-mail

phone *fax*

NAME

address

e-mail

phone *fax*

NAME

address

e-mail

phone *fax*

NAME

address

e-mail

phone *fax*

NAME

address

e-mail

phone *fax*

NAME

address

e-mail

phone *fax*

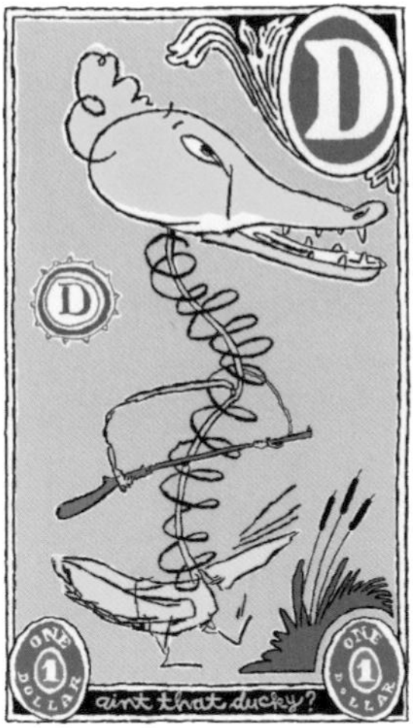

D

D

is for

DUCK STAMPS

Issued by the US Fish and Wildlife Service every year to validate duck hunting licenses. Designs are chosen in an open competition, and many collectors consider these the most handsome stamps produced in the US. Once applied to a license, the stamp must be signed by the bearer.

NAME

address

e-mail

phone *fax*

NAME

address

e-mail

phone *fax*

NAME

address

e-mail

phone *fax*

NAME

address

e-mail

phone *fax*

NAME

address

e-mail

phone *fax*

NAME

address

e-mail

phone *fax*

NAME

address

e-mail

phone *fax*

NAME

address

e-mail

phone *fax*

NAME

address

e-mail

phone *fax*

NAME

address

e-mail

phone *fax*

NAME

address

e-mail

phone *fax*

NAME

address

e-mail

phone *fax*

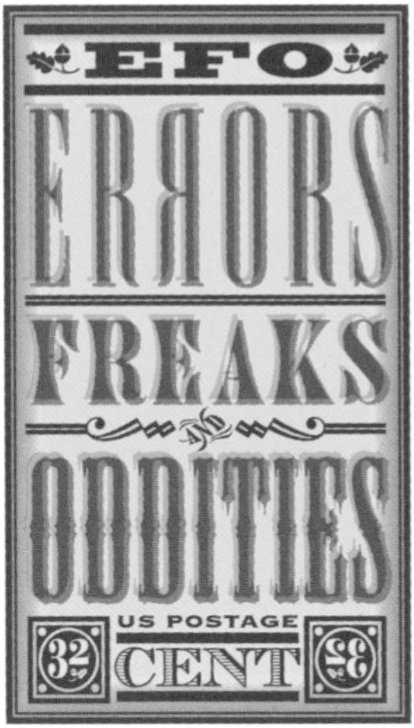

E

E

is for

E F O' S

Misprints, misperfs, and other production blunders. The initials stand for Errors, Freaks, and Oddities. Perforations shouldn't run through the middle of the design; grass shouldn't be blue; 2-cent stamps shouldn't say "5 cents." However, all of these errors have occurred on US stamps, and collectors love them.

NAME

address

e-mail

phone *fax*

NAME

address

e-mail

phone *fax*

NAME

address

e-mail

phone *fax*

NAME

address

e-mail

phone *fax*

NAME

address

e-mail

phone *fax*

NAME

address

e-mail

phone *fax*

NAME

address

e-mail

phone *fax*

NAME

address

e-mail

phone *fax*

NAME

address

e-mail

phone *fax*

NAME

address

e-mail

phone *fax*

NAME

address

e-mail

phone *fax*

NAME

address

e-mail

phone *fax*

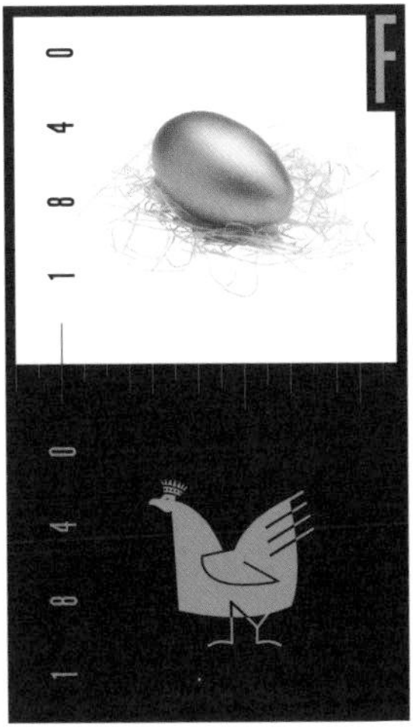

F

F

is for

FIRST

Stamp collectors love philatelic firsts. The US issued its first triangular stamps in 1997. First Day Covers and First Flight Covers are perennial collecting favorites. A challenging and expensive specialty is the first stamp issued by each country, starting with the first stamp worldwide, Great Britain's "Penny Black" of 1840.

NAME

address

e-mail

phone *fax*

NAME

address

e-mail

phone *fax*

NAME

address

e-mail

phone *fax*

NAME

address

e-mail

phone *fax*

NAME

address

e-mail

phone *fax*

NAME

address

e-mail

phone *fax*

NAME

address

e-mail

phone *fax*

NAME

address

e-mail

phone *fax*

NAME

address

e-mail

phone *fax*

NAME

address

e-mail

phone *fax*

NAME

address

e-mail

phone *fax*

NAME

address

e-mail

phone *fax*

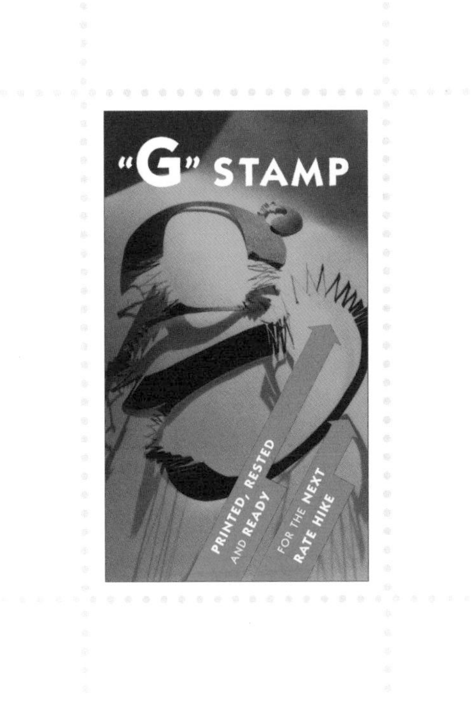
"G" STAMP
PRINTED, RESTED AND READY
FOR THE NEXT RATE HIKE

G

is for

"G" STAMP

The 1994 edition in the series of non-denominated US alphabet stamps. None will win a design competition, but each has aided a transition to new postal rates in the US. We've had "A" (1978) through "H" (1999). Expect "I" by 2002. (Let's all scream for ice cream!)

NAME

address

e-mail

phone *fax*

NAME

address

e-mail

phone *fax*

NAME

address

e-mail

phone *fax*

NAME

address

e-mail

phone *fax*

NAME

address

e-mail

phone *fax*

NAME

address

e-mail

phone *fax*

NAME

address

e-mail

phone *fax*

NAME

address

e-mail

phone *fax*

NAME

address

e-mail

phone *fax*

NAME

address

e-mail

phone *fax*

NAME

address

e-mail

phone *fax*

NAME

address

e-mail

phone *fax*

MAY

H

is for

HAND-STAMP

Any postal marking applied with a hand-held stamp and inkpad. Fancy cancels, pointing hands, and messages such as "Return to Sender" and "Received Without Contents" are examples. Rarely used in today's highly automated postal world, they were common and varied until the turn of the twentieth century.

NAME

address

e-mail

phone *fax*

NAME

address

e-mail

phone *fax*

NAME

address

e-mail

phone *fax*

NAME

address

e-mail

phone *fax*

NAME

address

e-mail

phone *fax*

NAME

address

e-mail

phone *fax*

NAME

address

e-mail

phone *fax*

NAME

address

e-mail

phone *fax*

NAME

address

e-mail

phone *fax*

NAME

address

e-mail

phone *fax*

NAME

address

e-mail

phone *fax*

NAME

address

e-mail

phone *fax*

32¢
IN·VERT:
TO TURN
INSIDE OUT
OR UPSIDE
DOWN

I

is for

INVERT ERROR

A stamp with part of its design printed upside down. The most famous and valuable example is the Inverted Jenny, which occurred on the first US airmail stamp in 1918. The central image—a Curtiss Jenny biplane—is upside-down.

NAME

address

e-mail

phone | *fax*

NAME

address

e-mail

phone | *fax*

NAME

address

e-mail

phone | *fax*

NAME

address

e-mail

phone *fax*

NAME

address

e-mail

phone *fax*

NAME

address

e-mail

phone *fax*

NAME

address

e-mail

phone *fax*

NAME

address

e-mail

phone *fax*

NAME

address

e-mail

phone *fax*

NAME

address

e-mail

phone | *fax*

NAME

address

e-mail

phone | *fax*

NAME

address

e-mail

phone | *fax*

EMISSION JOINT ISSUE
CONJOINTE

J
is for
JOINT ISSUE

Similar stamps issued concurrently by two or more countries. To celebrate the Statue of Liberty's 100TH birthday in 1986, the US and France each issued a stamp depicting Lady Liberty. In 1992, the 500TH anniversary of Columbus's voyages, four countries cooperated to issue commemorative sets of souvenir sheets. This recent form of international collaboration is becoming increasingly popular.

NAME

address

e-mail

phone *fax*

NAME

address

e-mail

phone *fax*

NAME

address

e-mail

phone *fax*

NAME

address

e-mail

phone *fax*

NAME

address

e-mail

phone *fax*

NAME

address

e-mail

phone *fax*

NAME

address

e-mail

phone *fax*

NAME

address

e-mail

phone *fax*

NAME

address

e-mail

phone *fax*

NAME

address

e-mail

phone *fax*

NAME

address

e-mail

phone *fax*

NAME

address

e-mail

phone *fax*

K
TOWN
1914
KANSAS
CITY ROULETTE

K

is for

KANSAS CITY ROULETTES

Specially perforated stamps created in 1914 by the postmaster of Kansas City, who wanted to sell his surplus supply of imperforates. He bought a seamstress's tracing wheel, scored a stack of sheets, then broke them apart and sold them. Usually collected in blocks of four, they are scarce and valuable.

NAME

address

e-mail

phone *fax*

NAME

address

e-mail

phone *fax*

NAME

address

e-mail

phone *fax*

NAME

address

e-mail

phone *fax*

NAME

address

e-mail

phone *fax*

NAME

address

e-mail

phone *fax*

NAME

address

e-mail

phone *fax*

NAME

address

e-mail

phone *fax*

NAME

address

e-mail

phone *fax*

NAME

address

e-mail

phone *fax*

NAME

address

e-mail

phone *fax*

NAME

address

e-mail

phone *fax*

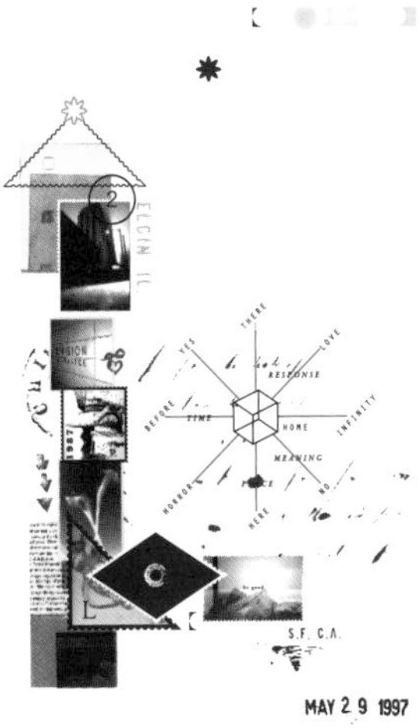
ELGIN IL.
THERE
LOVE
YES
RESPONSE
BEFORE
TIME
HOME
INFINITY
MEANING
HORROR
PEACE
NO
HERE
S.F. C.A.
MAY 29 1997

L

is for

LOCAL POSTS

The bicycle messengers of yesteryear. Up until the 1860s, US mail service operated only between post offices. Private companies offered pickup and delivery within larger cities, and some of them created their own stamps to show payment of fees.

NAME

address

e-mail

phone | *fax*

NAME

address

e-mail

phone | *fax*

NAME

address

e-mail

phone | *fax*

NAME

address

e-mail

phone *fax*

NAME

address

e-mail

phone *fax*

NAME

address

e-mail

phone *fax*

NAME

address

e-mail

phone *fax*

NAME

address

e-mail

phone *fax*

NAME

address

e-mail

phone *fax*

NAME

address

e-mail

phone *fax*

NAME

address

e-mail

phone *fax*

NAME

address

e-mail

phone *fax*

MULREADY ENVELOPES

M

M

is for

MULREADY ENVELOPES

Elaborately decorated, pre-paid envelopes issued in England in 1840, at the same time as the first postage stamps. Their fanciful design was perceived by the public as condescending and even ridiculous, hence they saw little use and were withdrawn. Today they are popular, though expensive, collectibles.

Designed by Michael Osborne; Michael Osborne Design, San Francisco.

NAME

address

e-mail

phone *fax*

NAME

address

e-mail

phone *fax*

NAME

address

e-mail

phone *fax*

NAME

address

e-mail

phone *fax*

NAME

address

e-mail

phone *fax*

NAME

address

e-mail

phone *fax*

NAME

address

e-mail

phone *fax*

NAME

address

e-mail

phone *fax*

NAME

address

e-mail

phone *fax*

NAME

address

e-mail

phone *fax*

NAME

address

e-mail

phone *fax*

NAME

address

e-mail

phone *fax*

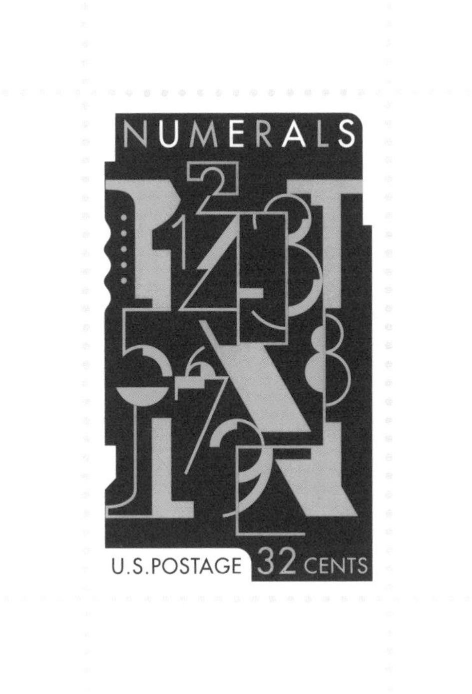
NUMERALS
U.S.POSTAGE
32 CENTS

N

is for

NUMERALS

The usual way of indicating a stamp's value as postage. Universal Postal Union regulations require that all stamps for international mail have Arabic numerals, hence our G-stamp and all the other alphabet stamps are invalid for such use (though "G" was the first to be inscribed "For U.S. addresses only"). Most countries have also used Roman numerals and spelled-out denominations.

NAME

address

e-mail

phone *fax*

NAME

address

e-mail

phone *fax*

NAME

address

e-mail

phone *fax*

NAME

address

e-mail

phone *fax*

NAME

address

e-mail

phone *fax*

NAME

address

e-mail

phone *fax*

NAME

address

e-mail

phone *fax*

NAME

address

e-mail

phone *fax*

NAME

address

e-mail

phone *fax*

NAME

address

e-mail

phone *fax*

NAME

address

e-mail

phone *fax*

NAME

address

e-mail

phone *fax*

O

is for

OVER-PRINT

Any text, numerals, or design element added to an existing stamp, thereby creating a new one. The new stamp may have a different value (such as the inflation-era stamps of Germany in the 1930s); a different meaning (such as the US's Hawaii commemorative of 1928); or even a different country (such as many recent stamps of former republics of the USSR).

NAME

address

e-mail

phone *fax*

NAME

address

e-mail

phone *fax*

NAME

address

e-mail

phone *fax*

NAME

address

e-mail

phone *fax*

NAME

address

e-mail

phone *fax*

NAME

address

e-mail

phone *fax*

NAME

address

e-mail

phone *fax*

NAME

address

e-mail

phone *fax*

NAME

address

e-mail

phone *fax*

NAME

address

e-mail

phone *fax*

NAME

address

e-mail

phone *fax*

NAME

address

e-mail

phone *fax*

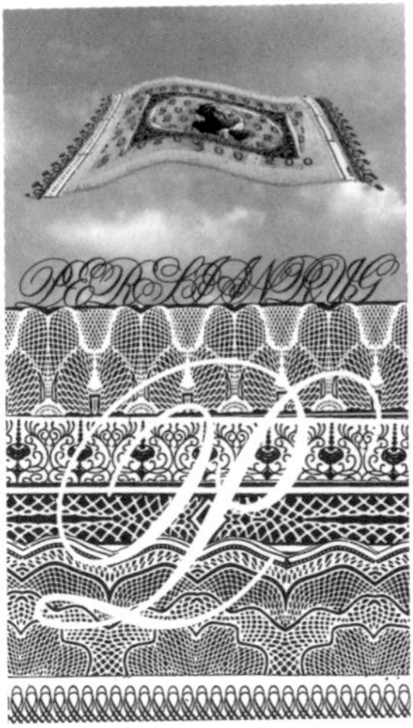
PERSIAN RUG

P

is for

PERSIAN RUG

The highest valued stamp ($500) in a series of documentary revenue stamps issued in 1871. (An even larger, more elaborate $5,000 value was designed but never issued.) Its large size, 2" x 4", and intricate, colorful design—more like currency than a stamp—prompted its nickname. Its current price is around $12,500; you wouldn't want to walk on it.

NAME

address

e-mail

phone | *fax*

NAME

address

e-mail

phone | *fax*

NAME

address

e-mail

phone | *fax*

NAME

address

e-mail

phone *fax*

NAME

address

e-mail

phone *fax*

NAME

address

e-mail

phone *fax*

NAME

address

e-mail

phone *fax*

NAME

address

e-mail

phone *fax*

NAME

address

e-mail

phone *fax*

NAME

address

e-mail

phone *fax*

NAME

address

e-mail

phone *fax*

NAME

address

e-mail

phone *fax*

Q

Q *is for* QUALITY

Another term for "condition," which, to the discerning stamp collector, is paramount. Factors that determine a stamp's quality include centering, perforations, impression, color, freshness, and cancellation. And, believe it or not, the condition of gum on stamps is so important that there's a profitable (though unethical) industry in regumming old stamps.

NAME

address

e-mail

phone *fax*

NAME

address

e-mail

phone *fax*

NAME

address

e-mail

phone *fax*

NAME

address

e-mail

phone *fax*

NAME

address

e-mail

phone *fax*

NAME

address

e-mail

phone *fax*

NAME

address

e-mail

phone *fax*

NAME

address

e-mail

phone *fax*

NAME

address

e-mail

phone *fax*

NAME

address

e-mail

phone *fax*

NAME

address

e-mail

phone *fax*

NAME

address

e-mail

phone *fax*

R
RAILWAY POST OFFICE
3

R

is for

RAILWAY POST OFFICE

A special mail car on a train. From the 1860s through the 1950s, most inter-city mail in the US was sorted and cancelled en route in these cars. In the 1960s and '70s, Highway Post Offices in buses did the job. The last RPO was shut down in 1977.

NAME

address

e-mail

phone *fax*

NAME

address

e-mail

phone *fax*

NAME

address

e-mail

phone *fax*

NAME

address

e-mail

phone *fax*

NAME

address

e-mail

phone *fax*

NAME

address

e-mail

phone *fax*

NAME

address

e-mail

phone *fax*

NAME

address

e-mail

phone *fax*

NAME

address

e-mail

phone *fax*

NAME

address

e-mail

phone | *fax*

NAME

address

e-mail

phone | *fax*

NAME

address

e-mail

phone | *fax*

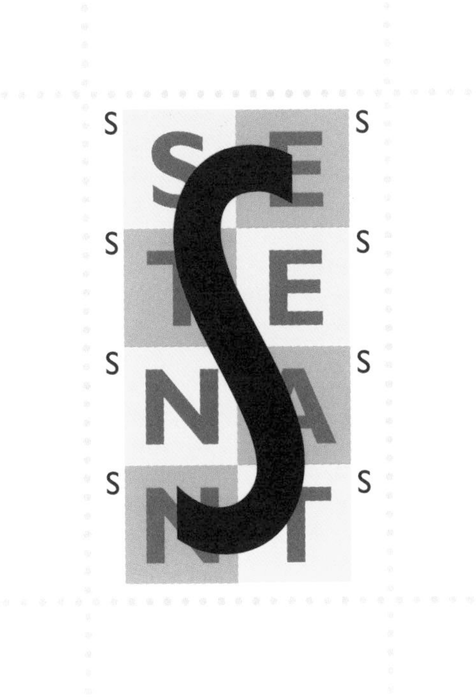
SE
TE
NA
NT
S S S S S S S S

S

is for

SETENANT

Two or more stamps on the same pane having different designs, denominations, or colors; from the French word meaning "joined." The first example in the US was a block of four holly stamps—the 1964 Christmas issue. An impressive example was the fifty-stamp sheet in 1976 representing all fifty state flags. Once rare, setenants are now the most common format for new stamp issues.

NAME

address

e-mail

phone *fax*

NAME

address

e-mail

phone *fax*

NAME

address

e-mail

phone *fax*

NAME

address

e-mail

phone *fax*

NAME

address

e-mail

phone *fax*

NAME

address

e-mail

phone *fax*

NAME

address

e-mail

phone *fax*

NAME

address

e-mail

phone *fax*

NAME

address

e-mail

phone *fax*

NAME

address

e-mail

phone | *fax*

NAME

address

e-mail

phone | *fax*

NAME

address

e-mail

phone | *fax*

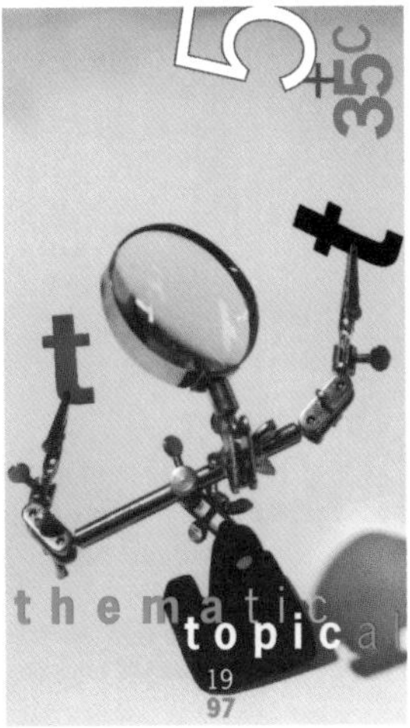
5
+35c
t
t
thematic
topical
19
97

T

is for

TOPICALS

Stamps relating to a single topic or theme, such as birds or trains or household appliances. This is a popular style of collecting, partly because there are few rules restricting it. Lightning, murder, and paperclips are among the unlikely subjects people have sought, and found, on stamps.

NAME

address

e-mail

phone *fax*

NAME

address

e-mail

phone *fax*

NAME

address

e-mail

phone *fax*

NAME

address

e-mail

phone *fax*

NAME

address

e-mail

phone *fax*

NAME

address

e-mail

phone *fax*

NAME

address

e-mail

phone *fax*

NAME

address

e-mail

phone *fax*

NAME

address

e-mail

phone *fax*

NAME

address

e-mail

phone *fax*

NAME

address

e-mail

phone *fax*

NAME

address

e-mail

phone *fax*

URANIA
oUranos
UNIVERSAL POSTAL UNION

U

is for

UNIVERSAL POSTAL UNION

A worldwide alliance of postal administrations, whose purpose is to regulate international mail by establishing standards and procedures for rates, accounting, and so forth. Established in 1874, it is an outstanding example of international cooperation. Member nations have issued many stamps honoring the UPU.

NAME

address

e-mail

phone *fax*

NAME

address

e-mail

phone *fax*

NAME

address

e-mail

phone *fax*

NAME

address

e-mail

phone | *fax*

NAME

address

e-mail

phone | *fax*

NAME

address

e-mail

phone | *fax*

NAME

address

e-mail

phone | *fax*

NAME

address

e-mail

phone | *fax*

NAME

address

e-mail

phone | *fax*

NAME

address

e-mail

phone *fax*

NAME

address

e-mail

phone *fax*

NAME

address

e-mail

phone *fax*

V

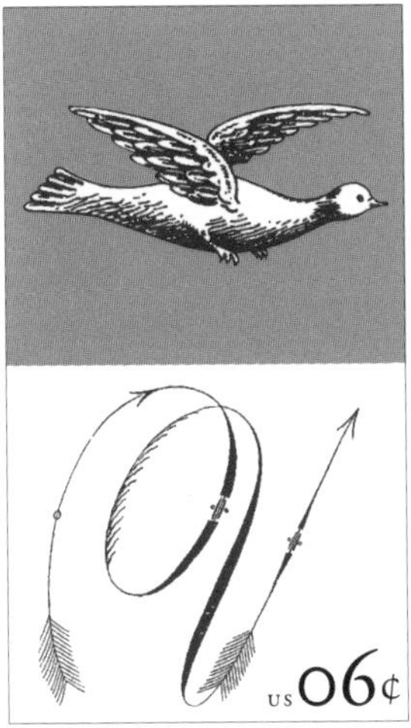

V

is for

V-MAIL

A mail photocopying system employed by the US during World War II. Letters to and from servicemen abroad were microfilmed on the sending end, then re-enlarged and printed on the receiving end. One roll of film weighing about seven ounces could hold over 1,500 letters, saving precious space and weight on transoceanic flights. Several billion letters were sent via V-mail between 1942 and 1945.

NAME

address

e-mail

phone *fax*

NAME

address

e-mail

phone *fax*

NAME

address

e-mail

phone *fax*

NAME

address

e-mail

phone *fax*

NAME

address

e-mail

phone *fax*

NAME

address

e-mail

phone *fax*

NAME

address

e-mail

phone *fax*

NAME

address

e-mail

phone *fax*

NAME

address

e-mail

phone *fax*

NAME

address

e-mail

phone *fax*

NAME

address

e-mail

phone *fax*

NAME

address

e-mail

phone *fax*

W

W *is for* WAR ISSUES

Specialized stamps and usages created by the pressures of war. Wars put a great strain on the postal services of their time, creating interesting specialties for stamp collectors. The Civil War gave rise to encased postage and many types of adversity covers; WWI saw the first widespread use of official censors' marks; and WWII gave us V-mail and the post-war stamps of the Allied Military Government.

NAME

address

e-mail

phone *fax*

NAME

address

e-mail

phone *fax*

NAME

address

e-mail

phone *fax*

NAME

address

e-mail

phone *fax*

NAME

address

e-mail

phone *fax*

NAME

address

e-mail

phone *fax*

NAME

address

e-mail

phone *fax*

NAME

address

e-mail

phone *fax*

NAME

address

e-mail

phone *fax*

NAME

address

e-mail

phone *fax*

NAME

address

e-mail

phone *fax*

NAME

address

e-mail

phone *fax*

X

X

is for

"X"

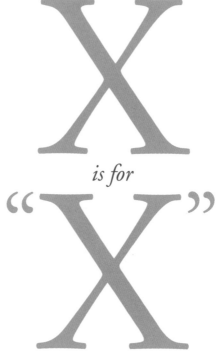

The letter X, as used on stamps and in postal services. It can be a manuscript cancel, for example, or the Roman numeral "10." Most collectors avoid stamps scrawled with "X" cancels, but these are sometimes the only surviving examples of rare early issues.

NAME

address

e-mail

phone *fax*

NAME

address

e-mail

phone *fax*

NAME

address

e-mail

phone *fax*

NAME

address

e-mail

phone *fax*

NAME

address

e-mail

phone *fax*

NAME

address

e-mail

phone *fax*

NAME

address

e-mail

phone *fax*

NAME

address

e-mail

phone *fax*

NAME

address

e-mail

phone *fax*

NAME

address

e-mail

phone | *fax*

NAME

address

e-mail

phone | *fax*

NAME

address

e-mail

phone | *fax*

DEPUIS 1887
Yvert & Tellier
REPUBLIQUE FRANÇAISE
5,00
CATALOGUE DE TIMBRES-POSTE

Y

is for

YVERT & TELLIER

The French company that publishes French-language stamp catalogs for the entire world. It also offers a prestigious line of stamp-collecting supplies and accessories, such as albums, stock books, and the palest blue glassine envelopes. Yvert & Tellier's counterpart in the US is the Scott Publishing Co.; in Great Britain, it's Stanley Gibbons; and in Germany, it's Michel.

NAME

address

e-mail

phone *fax*

NAME

address

e-mail

phone *fax*

NAME

address

e-mail

phone *fax*

NAME

address

e-mail

phone *fax*

NAME

address

e-mail

phone *fax*

NAME

address

e-mail

phone *fax*

NAME

address

e-mail

phone | *fax*

NAME

address

e-mail

phone | *fax*

NAME

address

e-mail

phone | *fax*

NAME

address

e-mail

phone *fax*

NAME

address

e-mail

phone *fax*

NAME

address

e-mail

phone *fax*

Z

Z

is for

ZEPPELIN POST

Transport of mail by zeppelin. From its start in 1910 until the fiery death of the Hindenburg in 1937, zeppelin air flight amazed and enchanted the world. Among the many stamps used on mail-carrying zeppelin flights is a set of three US stamps issued in 1930. Their current price ($1000 for a decent, unused set) is significantly lower than in the 1980s, when speculation inflated prices to astronomical heights.

Designed by Courtney Reeser, Jamie Calderon; Landor Associates, San Francisco.

NAME

address

e-mail

phone *fax*

NAME

address

e-mail

phone *fax*

NAME

address

e-mail

phone *fax*

NAME

address

e-mail

phone *fax*

NAME

address

e-mail

phone *fax*

NAME

address

e-mail

phone *fax*

NAME

address

e-mail

phone *fax*

NAME

address

e-mail

phone *fax*

NAME

address

e-mail

phone *fax*

NAME

address

e-mail

phone *fax*

NAME

address

e-mail

phone *fax*

NAME

address

e-mail

phone *fax*

NOTES NOTES NOTES NOTES NOTES NOTES

NOTES NOTES NOTES NOTES NOTES NOTES